What
Is
God?

◆◆◆ *To the children
of the world*

Edited by Jean-Jacques van Belle

"What is God?"

© 1989 Copyright by IPP Ltd.
International Promotions & Publications
Altona, Manitoba—London UK—Monterey, California

First edition

ISBN 0-88925-931-3

Type Univers

Printed and bound in Canada
by DW Friesen, Altona, Manitoba
Phone (204) 324-6401
Fax (204) 324-1333

What Is God?

by Etan Boritzer + illustrated by Robbie Marantz

Publisher's Note

Sometimes great things happen by accident. Hollywood is the last place you'd expect to find the author of a book called "What is God?", but Etan Boritzer and I met there by accident. Shortly thereafter, while leafing through Time magazine, I came across a terrific illustration by Robbie Marantz. I sent her the manuscript of our book and the next day she agreed to do the illustrations.

Bernice Barth, head librarian of Hawthorne Elementary School in Beverly Hills, gave us valuable advice regarding the editing of the book. By accident, we discovered that Robbie, who now lives in New York City, is an alumnus of Hawthorne Elementary School. Coincidence?

"What is God?" is a book for children. But children also need food, clothes, and shelter. UNICEF helps underprivileged children get the basics. The publishers, the author and the illustrator also want to help children through UNICEF.

Jean-Jacques Van Belle.

From the creator of Dennis The Menace

"Well, God, I goofed again."

...your unbiassed approach to the question
"What is God?"
is refreshing and stimulating. It may well be
useful to parents, teachers and youngsters...

Hank Ketcham.

hat is God?"
You are asking a very, very big question!
Boys and girls, grown-ups and old people,
Everyone wants to know "What is God?"

People who live in forests and mountains,
People who live in deserts, in cities, on farms,
Everyone wants to know "What is God?"

Maybe we can't really talk about God
Because maybe we can't see God
Or maybe we can't hear God
Or even taste or smell or touch God!

Maybe we can only feel God
Like we can feel love
Or like we can feel happy or sad.

maybe God is what you feel
When you stand on a very high mountain
And see a big beautiful view all around you.

Or maybe God is what you feel
When you hear beautiful music,
Sometimes soft, sometimes loud.

Or maybe God is what you feel
When you see a million stars at night
And you feel very small looking up at them.

Maybe we can feel God
When there is loud thunder
Or bright lightning outside our windows.

Long ago, people thought that the sun was God,
Like a very strong and great light
That shines through and around everything.

But now, we know that the sun is just one star
And really just one small star
In a big universe filled with millions of stars.

A universe is everything!
A universe is everything you can see
When you look up at the stars at night.

aybe God is an eternal mystery.
Eternal means forever and ever,
And a mystery is like a big puzzle,
With lots of pieces you have to fit together.

Is there anyone who can really tell us,
How all the many pieces of this big,
And forever puzzle called God fit together?

Some people think that there are teachers,
Who have been able to solve the puzzle
"What is God?"
These teachers, men, women, and even children
Have come from many places in the world
And have talked in many different languages,
About the question, "What is God?"

Some people think that God is an old man,
With a long white beard
Who sits up in the clouds
And looks down at us all the time.

They think that this God knows everything,
Everything we do, or say, or even think,
And when some people talk about this God
They look up at the clouds toward Him.

Sometimes this God is a nice old man
But sometimes this God is an angry old man
And some people think that if we are not good,
This God will be angry with us.

Next time you fly in an airplane,
Look out the window at the clouds.
But you won't see that God there,
Because no one has ever seen that God!

Some of these teachers still live today
But most of the great teachers lived long ago,
And people passed their teachings along,
To their children, and so on.

This passing on of the teachings,
Went on for many, many years,
And that's how many religions got started.

A religion is a belief held by a group of people
Who all understand God in the same way,
Usually, as one teacher taught them about God.

People of the Christian religion
Understand God as the teacher Jesus Christ
Taught them about God.

People of the Jewish religion
Understand God as the teacher Moses
Taught them about God.

People of the Muslim religion
Understand God as the teacher Mohammed
Taught them about God.

People of the Buddhist religion
Understand God as the teacher Buddha
Taught them about God.

And there are many, many more teachers,
Who have taught many, many different people,
Many, many different things about God!

But if there are so many different ways
To learn about the forever puzzle of God,
How can we ever begin to understand God?

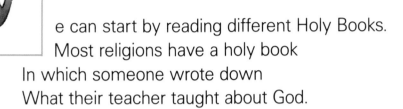

We can start by reading different Holy Books.
Most religions have a holy book
In which someone wrote down
What their teacher taught about God.

People of the Christian religion read
A holy book called the Bible.
People of the Muslim religion read
A holy book called the Koran.

People of the Jewish religion read
A holy book called the Torah.
Buddhists read the Sutras,
While Hindu people read the Vedas.

Y ou see, every religion is different,
And people of every religion understand God
In their own different way.

Sometimes, people of one religion want everyone
To know "What is God?" in the same way
That they understand God.

Sometimes, people of one religion,
Don't like people of another religion
Just because their religion is different,
Or they don't understand the other religion.

And sometimes, people of one religion start fights
With people of another religion
Because they don't understand that
Most religions are almost the same!

How are most religions almost the same?
Most religions teach that you should be good
To other people, just like you would want
Other people to be good to you!

Most religions say that you should not lie,
Most religions say that you should not steal,
Most religions say you should not hurt people.
There are many ways all religions are the same.

If everyone thought about all the ways
In which all the different religions are the same,
Maybe people wouldn't have so many fights,
About all the different answers to the question,
"What is God?"

raying is a way to try
To talk to God,
And people of all religions pray.

When people pray, they try to talk to God,
From very deep in their hearts,
About something that is very important to them.

People pray to God in many different ways.
People pray while sitting, or standing,
Or they pray by reading from their holy book.

And people of different religions
Pray in many different places called
Churches, or synagogues, or mosques, or temples.

But you can really pray anywhere,
By your bed, or in a park, or on a mountain,
As long as when you pray you really mean it!

But wait!
We have only talked about the big religions.
There are many people who believe
That there are many Gods,
Not just one God.

And there are some places in the world
Where you are not allowed to talk about God,
And where there are no places allowed,
To even pray to God.

But in our country,
We believe that everybody can pray,
According to his or her religion.
And everybody is allowed to ask,
"What is God?"

There are many ways to talk about God.
Does that mean that everything
That everybody ever says about God is right?
Does that mean that God is everything?

Yes! God is everything great and small!
God is everything far away and near!
God is everything bright and dark!
And God is everything in between!

If everything is God,
God is the last leaf on a tree,
If everything is God,
God is an elephant crashing through the jungle.

If everything is God,
Then God is the hot wind in the desert,
And God is the freezing snow in the winter,
And God is the big, yellow moon.

If everything is God,
Then I am God,
You are God,
All of us are God!

S o when we pray to God,
When people of all religions pray to God,
We are really praying for that feeling,
The feeling which connects all of us.

When we pray to God,
We are praying for that feeling of love
To come to us and to everybody we know,
Maybe even to all those people we don't know,
So that we can all be happy together, or apart.

And if you really want to pray to God,
You can just close your eyes anywhere,
And think about that feeling of God,
That makes you part of everything and everybody.

If you can feel that feeling of God,
And everybody else can feel that feeling of God,
Then we can all become friends together,
And we can really understand,
"What is God?"

S o, if you really want to feel God,
  You can close your eyes now,
And listen to your breath go slowly in and out,
And think how you are connected to everything,
Even if you are not touching everything.

Try to feel how you are connected
To your Dad, and how you are part of your Mom,
Try to feel how you are part of your whole family,
Like your brother or sister, your grandparents,
Your aunt or uncle, cousins, even your friends.

And try to feel how all of those people,
Are part of a whole bigger family,
And how all the families of the world,
(Even those we can't see or touch),
Are really a part of you and your family.

And if you can start to feel God like that,
Then maybe you will soon feel the whole answer,
To that very, very big question that everyone asks,
"What is God?"